STAGES OF TANNING WORDS AND REMEMBERING SPELLS

TAWAHUM BIGE

STAGES of TANNING WORDS and REMEMBERING SPELLS

Part 1: SCRAPING LUNGS LIKE HIDE

NIGHTWOOD EDITIONS
2025

1 2 3 4 5 — 29 28 27 26 25

Nightwood Editions
P.O. Box 1779
Gibsons, BC V0N 1V0
Canada
www.nightwoodeditions.com

COVER ART: Jonas Bige
COVER DESIGN: Libris Simas Ferraz / Onça Publishing
TYPOGRAPHY: Rafael Chimicatti

Nightwood Editions acknowledges the support of the Canada Council for the Arts, the Government of Canada, and the Province of British Columbia through the BC Arts Council.

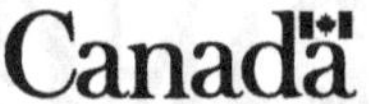

Canada Council for the Arts Conseil des Arts du Canada

This book has been printed on 100% post-consumer recycled paper.

Printed and bound in Canada.

LIBRARY AND ARCHIVES CANADA CATALOGUING IN PUBLICATION

Title: Stages of tanning words and remembering spells. Part 1,
Scraping lungs like hide / Tawahum Bige.
Other titles: Scraping lungs like hide
Names: Bige, Tawahum, author.
Identifiers: Canadiana (print) 2025012288X | Canadiana (ebook) 20250122987 |
ISBN 9780889714601 (softcover) | ISBN 9780889714618 (EPUB)
Subjects: LCGFT: Poetry.
Classification: LCC PS8603.I3835 S73 2025 | DDC C811/.6—dc23

CONTENTS

CRY

verb
to shed tears often noisily

"The baby had to cry until the mother reached out and held them, if the mother did so."

noun
a loud inarticulate shout or scream expressing a powerful feeling or emotion

"When in a place, far from home and surrounded by white walls, all he could let out was a cry."

i used to cry, then i didn't,
now i cry more than i ever did
cheesy 80s floral-printed duvet covers
on my bed at six years old
as i bawled and cried and sobbed
then suddenly awoke hours later

Bread Bag

She wouldn't let me play videogames.
Kneeling beside my single-sized mattress,
five years old, opening the storage bed drawer.
Packing pants, pajamas, t-shirts—
I'mma get my hobo pack and get on out of here—
a loaf of white Wonder Bread
a dozen slices and I'm set.
I'm running away!

Mom smiles, laughs.
Go ahead.

I stand.
I hate you!

Well, I don't like you very much right now either.
I finish packing, her face unfazed:
Door's that way.
All I needed was for her to care.

I got down the stairs.
I got down the hallway.
I was at the door, this way.
Couldn't do it,
collapsed in my tears,
Momma with a smirk,
wide to her left ear.

I can't go anywhere.

Making a Nerd, or How My Dad Ranted About How the Elves Never Showed Up at Helm's Deep in *The Two Towers* Directed by Peter Jackson

after Julian Randall

Couple days after winter solstice,
my dad took me to see *The Two Towers.*
We biked, maybe walked, also bussed
across Newton to Scottsdale Cineplex   to catch up
to his young adulthood in the bathtub
where he first read *The Lord of the Rings.*
I don't know if I was excited for the fantasy
or to enter this fantasy with him,   boy and man.
There were moments   clear in a swift sunrise
of tree-people and castle keeps and hills rolling
into my dad's waking dream. The way the projector
lit his face, shine reflecting off glasses
and I can't remember if he piled popcorn
into his mouth or not   salivating like eager eyes.
We left the theatre   and I felt so close
to him and his outstretched palm
full of a one-magic-gold-ring joy not often found
in our six-person-peasant-home. He talked and talked
of this production quality   and he talked and talked
on Tolkien and these halflings   and he talked and talked
to tell me how the Elves never protected the Men
and the Men did it   all alone against overwhelming odds,
and I know   he wishes he could protect us   all alone
against overwhelming odds.

The quick walk   followed us
to the Chapters bookstore in Newton
and the journey   back to low-income townhouse;
so much son   amongst so much father.

Stress Headaches and White Flashes

The double futon in the front room leaves me sore.
I sleep here but wouldn't call it a bedroom.   Hot water tank.
    No door.   Window is a glass pane that doesn't open.
  Harry Potter jokes and I even got the lightning-bolt tattoo.
    Curtain in the doorway separates storage from kitty-litter box.
Who the fuck calls it senior year? Grade twelve. Graduation year
and my bedroom isn't mine anymore.   I don't cry there
and I certainly don't cry in the front room.   My dad sleeps
in the living room and I ain't trying to let anyone hear nothin'.
    Just holding that sob in for days, weeks, months, until
      one day I hear a voice telling me to do chores,
    or I get home from school and am getting ready for work
or we go to a wedding as a whole family   or I'm laying my head
down at three a.m. to maybe sleep, finally—

                              when an M84 stun grenade detonates my brain—
    my ears can hear the white flash, my eyes see nothing but ringing
      cover the sides of my head,   not crying but teary-eyed and waiting
and waiting   and waiting.   I'm sure I drank enough water.

I don't tell anyone about this.
    At least, not until that Baptist wedding and it takes me
in the middle seat between siblings (despite being youngest).
No one really cares or notices
    except my sister. She cares.

I remember pre-drinking
at her place then we went to her boyfriend's weird band
in Fort Langley
with the buffalo skull logo and when we finish dancing
and return to her home she asks about family
she asks about the headaches
I am suddenly a faucet, a hot crying mess
and she gets it, because she went through it.
Now it's exposition and I can't stand it.
I bawled, yeah. White flash headaches, yeah.
Never stopped, yeah. I mean it did one day.
Graduation finishes, I pay rent for that dilapidation
and after drinking myself stupid
and a friend who says he thinks it's shitty
that I have to be so quiet in my own bedroom
so I don't wake my dad,
I get up one day,
quit the bottle for a second (six months),
save up, and move the fuck out.

another poem about not getting out of bed

it's especially bad
after less than six hours sleep
scrolling through Instagram feeds
screen-fed narratives
and wanting to be noticed
or for breakfast to already be made
and Spotify to play my stupid little playlist
without me having to do any of it

a poem on crying in my sleep:
at three a.m., I read a nonfic on trauma healing
then I dreamt my friends abandoned me.
feeling alone again in the risen sunlight
pushing the shades of broken branches
onto my ceiling, intrusive thoughts sounding truthful
and now I can't stand sleeping
can't stand to be awake
can I just stay home today?

this poem is for rough days despite sunlight:
the wooden canvas on my wall etched in violets & greens
& yellows & teals doesn't hold me
but I dissociate into Cody Lecoy's painting regardless.
remember breathing. remember speaking.
it's a walk in the sunlight,
outside, outdoors, out there,
with headphones & oranges & blues
from skies to barely hold me through.

my poem of open endings:
if I chose my own adventure
would I still be in bed over an hour after
waking? is it the screen I type this on?
or the fact that I wake alone
and alone and alone
and I'm always so fucking mean to myself
and I'm always tired every morning
three hours, six hours, twelve hours—
I get up when I have to.
which is to say pigeon cooing
garbage truck banging
coffee press brewing
Google calendar inviting
become my reasons to endure waking up—

I wish I had my own fucking reason
to endure waking up.

Attention Deficit

Give me a breather. A spare lung. Some way out.
Need to quit smoking. Finish my degree. Mend
complex trauma wounds. Learn guitar. To cook.
A drum beats in the distance. I masturbate.
A drum beats in the distance. I come undone.
A drum beats in the distance. Edging is a gift
to get me out of bed. I've since taken a metal
detector to deep wounds. I've dug up treasure
troves, struck gold, kept going. Workshop
weekends. Smoked up. Waited to hear her voice.
Do I make it up? Contrive crush to soothe scars.
Do I make it up? Convince myself it will work out.
Do I make it up for a good story or bad
romance or do I gaslight my own ass
because I'm scared of rejection—only,
my spirit puffs his chest up and I am still here.
I rarely see my siblings anymore. I drank
whiskey, once. I've forgotten to water my plants,
kept them so far out of sunlight they began to wilt,
still alive. I grind my coffee for the French press
the night before. Except when I don't.
I've wasted hours taking selfies & editing shirtless
pictures I won't show anyone.
I confess a lot. God never gave me penance.
I confess a lot. I still drag my name thru the muck.
I confess a lot. And I didn't even do it.
The bad thing. The wrong note. The razor
over my wrist—I didn't even do it.
I wonder how much art I have made

out of my own Sistine Chapel. Out
of my own collapsing Notre-Dame—it's on brand
for me to self-sabotage while others are contracted
to help me rebuild. How the art revels in the ashes
of a rejected Catholicism. I'm scared
of rejection. Of quitting smoking. I rarely
see my siblings anymore. Do I make it up?
Smoked up. God never gave me penance. The
wrong note. For a good story or bad romance.
A drum beats in the distance. Waited to hear
her voice. I confess a lot. Grind my coffee
for the French press the night before. Kept
them so far out of sunlight, editing
shirtless pics I won't show anyone.
I drank whiskey once, or do I gaslight
my own ass. Gift to get me out of bed.
Struck gold. Learn guitar. Some way out.
Out of my own Sistine Chapel. Out of my own
collapsing Notre-Dame. I really want to show
this to her. How the art revels in the ashes.
It's on brand for me to self-sabotage.
I come undone. Some way out. A spare lung.
I still drag my name thru the muck.
Except when I don't.

Sanctum

after Julian Randall

It went like this: I became stuck in that room. When I say, stuck in that room, I mean the room was all holes. I wasn't crawling out of the holes, I was rummaging a maze of tunnels—my grief, stricken long before I lost my brother. I scoured drywall cavern through 'til then. Hit me about five weeks in—I wasn't going to pass my classes, though I always took my meds. The basement suite: my mansion, the playhouse, a home for this clown. I could tell the October day by the sticky taste of lemon haze from my orange pipe; I held my breath for two years underground. I lived behind the cemetery, and below. The room turned grave; I slept. Depression: in bed, on the computer, with friends or playing games. Manipulation: she only climbed into this hole with me for so many repeated visits before I made her leave. I coughed more than I admit. With anyone in this hole with me, I realized how little I wanted to remain. Stopped dreaming; fantasies blinked on computer display instead. At night, streetlight fell down tunnels, pebbles, oak planks, ricocheted off windowsill and into blinds. I'm trying to say this underground, darkened, was still alight. Though, I remember power outages that lasted weeks. I praised the dark and slowly asphyxiated, rubble fumes thick on tongue and nostrils. The day only ever came in streaks of momentary blue. So, with at least a pack of cigarettes per day, I held ceremony embracing night. Plastic Safeway bag filled with butts and ash, gathering monument in the corner of the room. I dug deep using a rotation of shovels: videogames, cannabis, Dexedrine, sedatives and faithlessness. Couldn't respond to texts or call my sister back. Dropped my classes online, without leaving the pit. My funding cheque arrived for November; they didn't know. The valley between spine and shoulder blade felt sore again and again. Why was I majoring in information technology? At a young age I dreamt of living in a hole. Instead, sputtered life into a nightmare. An agoraphobic labyrinth I both transformed into and was trapped inside of. The gravel rattling unearthed my lungs gasping when I was excavated from those holes, and I cried dust, and dust, and dust.

sâkahikanisihk

mîtosak watch us in Green Timbers Park
I'm six years old   ohcî nohtawiy ekwa nimis
mîyoskaminihk   hunting
ayîkis   ayîkisis
whatever we could get the bucket on

grey sky   grey plight   golf cap   fall flat
right into the water   head to toe
I'm soaked   SOAKED
clothes a darker shade   of tan-coloured corduroy
and grey dress shirt   and my hat floats
I rise   tears welling   hyperventilating

hadda ask my sister at twenty-five   to find this out:

I am pointing
tâwakâmohk   sâkahikanisihk
choking out *my-my-my*   *my h-h-h m-m-my h-h-ha!*
she fished nitastotin out for me   but I am inconsolable
and so cold

nitahkapawen mistahi

WHIMPER

verb

to make a low whining plaintive or broken sound

"They whimper at the most inane and mundane of chores assigned to them, even emptying the kitty litter."

noun

a low, feeble sound expressive of fear or pain

"Being surrounded by hostile teenage boys outside the front door of Frank Hurt Secondary, he couldn't help but let out a whimper in every word spoken."

no one likes it when i whine
but i seem to always need to complain
even when things are going so very right in my life
i be thinking on words i heard growing up
life's a bitch and then you die
so i be bitchin' and moanin'
but it doesn't mean i'm not still having fun

Beggar

Wednesday Breakfast Club at Bear Creek Elementary
where I saw a bunch of Native kids (and others).
We joked and played, ate bagels and Raisin Bran.
My mom didn't like that I went: *We have food*
in the house. Didn't have anyone to play with at home
though, my siblings five, seven, ten years older.
I got to leap-frog   the generation gap   onto my own lily pad,
my siblings leaving the pond when I turned ten.
                                        I visited the other kids
at school in Breakfast Club   at lunchtime, I unwrapped
nothing.   Ate nothing.   Felt nothing.
                                        Mom stopped making lunches
after a grade two incident involving a backpack
wholly filled   with uneaten lunches.
I couldn't tell you why I didn't eat them.
There was food in the house but mornings were
rushed   *Quick*   *Hurry up*
Did you brush your teeth? Time for school.
                                                So I went lunch-less
and my friends thought I was poor(er than I was).

Crash and Spyro

Every day third grade, it's game time. All I can think about
waiting for school to end is Crash Bandicoot
and Spyro the Dragon,
my imaginary friends inside the PlayStation waiting for me
at home. I hammer that grey controller into creaky plastic
submission. My mom pokes her head into the living room,
Homework? Already did it, without a waver in my voice.
Lies and procrastination go together like Crash and Spyro—
they're made by the same companies, and everyone's played them—
the games I mean. The first person Crash and Spyro hurt
is me. In my head, I really did do my homework. I was smart
enough to not need a pen, paper, pencil, paper, pushpin, paper,
poking page. At school, I did my work like I play my games:
a speed-run to the finish while I could still focus on it.
Everything is a game. Fucking with the cats at home. Chores.
Unloading make-believe assault rifles at recess. *Bang bang.*
You always know if the invisible bullet makes contact. I always
know I didn't do my homework. Lies of omission? I just want to play.
My parents didn't like getting that eventual call, the missed
assignments, Ms. Nelson hadda tell them though. I play dumb
but sometimes that cat I fuck with tore a hole through
the sack. Doesn't matter how I whine, now I'm getting the full-check
after-school big-brother moment. Do my homework like I play
games. Do my chores like I play my games. Quick. To the end
of the stage. Learn the hack, the glitch, the workaround. Lie
better next time. Half-ass the homework. Pull out the page and speed-run
in the first five minutes of class starting. Hot damn I'm good at that.
I don't get detention for it 'til fifth grade. Treat the symptom,
not the problem. I do my lines in detention like I mastered

this videogame. The letter "I" drawn down the page 25 times over light-blue lines.

Refuse to write the sentence left to right. It goes letter by letter,

top to bottom. The game don't stop if you don't stop playing.

Crash and Spyro are parents to teach me how to move in this world

I can rely on.

Static.

Friendly.

Imaginary.

Chooser

On Monday, Tuesday and Thursday
I have two choices after school: play with my friends, hungry,
or head straight home to eat.
                                        I choose
toast and margarine; toast and peanut butter;
toast, peanut butter and jam;
toast sandwich, peanut butter and banana;
or toast sandwich, peanut butter, mayonnaise and pickle.
                        Wednesdays and Fridays, my parents choose
for me:
an after-school activity to earn allowance
(i.e.: money for Pop-Tarts, Cinnamon Toast Crunch,
Lunchables, Clodhoppers, sour keys).
So I deliver newspapers.

This Just In

I'm stomping behind Superstore during a snowstorm, dragging a red stand-up dolly attached to a rickety white gramma cart full of two-hundred-and-twenty-six *Surrey Leader* newspapers. Grunt, heave, *Whoa!* Good and bad news spill all over the alley, Christmas flyers fly upward, and I am upside-down. Powdered snow scent and soaked winter coat. Freezing tears sting; *I fucking quit.* Stack cart back up, hands cold, ink-stain texture from newspapers pierce numb fingertips.

The paperboy across the street stole my design. Sunshine, after school Wednesday, fun times funnelling into his delivery of *The Now* newspaper, Glencoe Estates across the street from Wedgewood. Black stand-up dolly and a silver-lining gramma cart, call it MacBook Pro–level innovation, and it's catching on with that red-headed paperboy. *Cheater.* I head into my complex, hulking cart in tow, with 99.3 "The Fox" on a little pocket radio and a headphone band that hurts my crown and temples, blasting the devil's tones.

Blue Eyes White Dragon

In a soccer mom's minivan headed for St. Bernadette's off 132nd. Her blonde-hair-blue-eyes-white-dragon boy with me in the back seat. I call him friend when he's not around until I learn he calls me weird when I'm not around. This is the first time I meet gossip, though they'd been talking about me long before.

We arrive, classroom lined with Mary, Joseph, Jesus, catechism children and our belief in God. Every Wednesday night a pastor-wannabe teacher teaches, *The spirits of the land and your ancestors are false idols; resist the temptation to curse even though your parents do constantly; Sundays are for resting unless it's still a workday; a dishonourable father must be honoured; don't kill but also don't ask about the crusades; the safest sex is abstinence and coveting your crush is a sin—so head on in for confession.* This room doesn't smell like anything. These sins were the taboos I worried about, while undiagnosed ADHD hyperactivity made me a taboo to be close enough for anyone to smell.

On the ride back, I'm tired. I deliver papers Wednesdays, Fridays and Sundays, a taboo job, the scent of musty crushed leaves in nostrils, wearing a water-soaked, ink-stained sweater and baggy jeans, as I pull my little gramma paper-cart down alleys and sidewalks into the senior's complex and then to the townhouses across from 138th Street. The wheels slip over fallen autumn leaves and my arms strengthen from heaving loads and dry heaving to keep balance.

Jumped

Two kids collide shin to shin and I'm writhing, crying and kicking on the gravel of the Bear Creek Elementary soccer field—Kurtis, this hulking, spiky-red-haired hero, carries me to the office. If I had walked it off on that left shin like the nurse had suggested it would've splintered into shards and screws. I didn't deliver newspapers for grade five summer.

When I get jumped in the alleyway of Wedgewood Estates, the weirdest part isn't that some kid is trying to steal a bundle of my papers, or that I'm still doing newspapers in grade nine. It isn't when I hear Rocky, the other Native boy in my grade, tell his friend, *Go, go, go!* or when I trip sliding into grass, giving chase, *Fuck!* It is that when I get up, and my push goes to shove Rocky's friend down, tasting metal in my mouth and hearing my plastic headphones drop to the ground, snapping like my leg on the soccer field: it's Kurtis who throws me to the concrete.

rosaries in hand

the purpose of a pulpit
translated to
hymns in chipewyan
heard in my territories

but in surrey
the purpose of a wink from mom
for slowing my feet
and hand movements
restless but still
the weight rests
on left leg
all kneel

how
straight collars
can teach choirs
the songs of wetako
medicine
the sick-making kind
fidgeting footwork
sermons from verses
on thin pages
all rise

the lord's lies be with you
and also with you
couples for christ
a lot of filipinx friends
youth for christ
catechism classrooms
you may be seated

is this family time?
pre-schizoaffective brother
or during
counting ceiling tiles
connecting triangles
in stained-with-our-shame
glass windows
red green blue
gold light running through
all rise

erasers gripped
indigenous lineage
in body
pinked out for
luminescent rosaries
and joseph mary
mini-statuettes
beads divine
glow-in-the-dark
all kneel

communion served
by a pastor visiting
my mother bed-ridden
saturday bike rides
to st. bernadette's
chain our shame
tires to pillars
on pebbled cement
walkways
all rise

for a hymn in english
another sermon
collections basket
extractions lasting
mental illness developing
sales of land
and refused apologies
all kneel

cushioned creed
pews and columns
make us pray
for our brain-waves
to align with their church
one day
y'all gonna be pissed
that i listen to death metal
all rise

confirmation day
oaths and anointment
red robes in our blood
and cash to purchase
this confirmation bias
i don't remember
seeing my brother there
you may be seated

youngest catholic
golden and gilded
child into post-baptism
post-communion
post-confirmation
teenager
all kneel

HOLLER

verb

to call out

"When pushed into a corner, they would holler into the bones of the pusher."

noun

a loud cry or shout

"Mess with his family, and you'll hear his holler."

fuck i yell a lot, wonder where i got it from
but the first thing i learned in life
was my greatest weapon is my voice
it will stop physical violence before it starts
but like any weapon
you don't learn how to carry it right
and you hurt yourself
you hurt the people closest to you

i haven't let myself holler in a decade

Voice

I scream *Fuck you* in the Chem 12 classroom
at the boys who jammed
my locker
and didn't do a good job

a moment before
walking Frank Hurt Secondary hallway
three boys surrounding pale-blue locker
I say, *Excuse me*
three mice jump
and sc at t er
giggling

I look at the lock *Oh*
long-haired skinny-jeaned emo-ass boy
used to the usual bull behaviour
I pull the lock comes out easily
shake head and chuckle under breath
at their attempt
toward contempt

the only amusement drawn
is from the target marked on my back

I get to my class and say, *If you wanna jam my lock*
maybe make it so I can't actually pull it out.
I hear back, *Yo shut up.* I hard-boil

my left hook doesn't exist
only uppercuts I know I've withstood
I carry only one weapon ever
and it is concealed in this lanky frame
only keen eyes might see
the jaw-width height how my chest rises
and sets the instrument closely nuzzled to my heart
warm blood ignites vocal chords

another day at lunch I holler,
Pick that fucking sandwich up!
My dad doesn't work his ass off
eight hours a day to pick up after
you! on the path through forest
at this boy between high school
and Surrey Newton townhouse
while my dad keeps the grounds
like an SD-36 groundskeeper does
on grassy hill under a silver sky

I am paces behind this boy
I am decibels above this boy
he does not look at me
but this little Oedipus motherfucker
picks up his motherfuckin' sandwich
and keeps on walkin'

my dad turns   his bald spot a hill
surrounded by grassy grey hair   glasses
but ain't seen or heard what happened
    instead just hears me yell,
    Love you dad!

he hollers back,
    I love you too!

Road Trip

nipawạtan wecîpweyânihk
nipihtos-mihko

ewîkiyân tahtwayak
ekwa âyiman

In the red family van between Summerland
and Surrey, we follow down the winding
highway around cliff
leading to any argument:
I hate this song—It's too loud.
I'm carsick—I hate you.
We don't change
the station, don't pull
over. We are slinging shit,
nothing cute about it.
Mom plays ref and judge
while dad is the loud,
red-faced Hungarian
bystander. We aren't there yet.
The highway curves and
we're left mountain-climbing,
granite-sliding summit & sin;
on the right, we're valley-dipping,
slope-declining, death trap
without a guardrail.

We'll be coming 'round the mountain when we come.

Inside our red Dodge van, the screaming ebbs.
The hesitation smells of charcoal.
Wood panelling peels a strip around
the middle of the vehicle carrying us
home. The Okanagan scrub-desert holds
shreds of brush-flame across miles.
My mom hasn't quit smoking, yet.
Argument ends with a cigarette butt
thrown from the window.
It's forest fire season.

reading comprehension

they think i'm not that bright
'til i turn on the light
switch
my vocab
esl office tested
reading
comprehension
instead of science lesson
grade eight
prove myself comprehensive

and them?
bright as coal
dimmest tool in the shed
they didn't notice my marks
grade seven – english – a
just saw that
ndn status
like no taxes
or free post-secondary access
or stupid fucking indian axis

my mom never understood
            "chug"
but before i comprehended
     "english as a second
             language"
she   let 'em have it
             racist battery acid
for settler energizer bunny
that keeps going and
going and
going
             to school

Ending Friendships

metawew
notinikew
masinahikew
pimâtasiw

I am a volcano
bubbling ash
crackling granite
dormant in cold winters—

I am charcoal clouds' only brightness,
the lightning and glow
from magma,
ruptured tectonics awaken—

I am this earthquake
shaking sternum to diamond
to mountains of rubble erupting,
I had hoped to hold off—

I am tunnels collapsing.
While geysers fill to the brim,
fire bellows to the surface
and this lava is—

I am peak exploding.
Make me devil with new mythos:
I fling megaliths like pebbles,
the way islands form is not gentle—

I am peninsula bridging
land splintering & emerging:
flame & soil, sorrow & steam
returning to transform—

You have left me revenant,
a territory unoccupied.
I grieve you living like I do
my lost brother and so many others—

And so today I am shifting terrain,
the cracks through boulder,
I fracture & reconnect
every bone to continent—

Comment-Thread Collapse

metawew
notinikew
masinahikew
pimâtasiw

My vulnerability is a breach in a crumbling stone wall,
ethics extracted from an archaeology of loss
excavated from escape tunnels where I am
silent in their collapse. I used to know army,
could glean tactical drone-strike from counting Likes,
an art of war from intuition.
I gathered my garrison of perfected politics,
air-quote correction swordplay,
cutting and slicing with deliberate
mercenary knife-work—

I made-believed that it was all for community—

but these were ramparts constructed by rage, mortar
and wrath. Radio-communications tower
broadcasts the basis of flawed rhetoric,
either calling in or out,
I sought the release of a demon
from a dungeon my conscience conferred with,
in secret, advice taken without question.
How the cobblestone creaks,

these castles based in architecture
bringing empire from foundation to cornerstone.
The veil is crumbling. The scaffolding scathes
into ruin, the militant reserve of troops inside
deserted me. I am contemplating collapse.
I have spent years playing with flag-pins on maps

drawn out of scale. My ruthlessness a refusal
to embody pain, to let tears drip rain down wall,
a refusal to walk away from a throne,
or cast-off mantles and medals of (dis)honour.
I have long since abandoned that old fortress

and wandered as the first man. I lost count
of how many castles I witnessed, owned by others
built over carnivorous demon caverns
housing their own whispering devourers
and consciences that listen—

my devourer travels with me, out in the open,
disbands my flawed conscience, throws down my arms.
Now I travel armed with only a pen.

There are rivers that flow undammed, still.
Networks of communities that know more
about gardening self and surrounding with support
than erecting wall and controlling with threats.

Now, on my better days, rage
is just a loud travelling companion
illuminating
the benefit of secure connection with my dark
so long as I hold it out and open,
rather than shamefully shaking hands
behind closed fortress gates.

Extinguishing Fires

locked up after
in prayer
boots on the ground

here now with you guards
that we
can't control

as if your uniform
your nightly patrol
your flashlight in window
your demand

you clang and clatter

of course
you ignore
you ignore
build up
when the power
I see
stitched into gloves

I say
you guards
between
me and
us and

sitting in a crosswalk
contempt
at the pipeline terminal

reminders
are here and
when I leave

my cell
my metal bed
my eyes covered
isn't more than enough

boots and keys

I bang
I yell
I start fires
the flame
goes out
in your hands
sweating palms

go to hell
with a steel door
you and
them and
I can't stop screaming

on the stairs and floors
our shared
rage and
uniform
wearing
dirty

for nineteen days
common ground
hate
power trips
our red slacks
covering my eyes at night

I hold
disrespect
for you
screaming

respect
from him
in his spit
in your face

consequences
a fit thrown
by powerless
escalations
paid by public dollar

whatever that means
in an unfit punishment
prisoners
reminders
to keep us subservient

you cops
you sheriffs
you guards
you wolves
of little pig little pig

in the precinct
at the court
of the prison
wearing the skin
contracted now

not blowing air
you erect
cinder brick by brick
iron bar by bar
clear-cut log by log

to knock the house down
around us
mortar and white paint
and the men who plant it
falling to the ground

we still bang
rattle
spark match to flint

for creature comforts
TVs
showers
phone calls

all of it takes thunder
but you
have it
on the other side of
segregated
divided

I start another fire
how else could it go
lock the door
while taking the credit
for problems you started
every night

on the wall
against the cage
there's no going back

no grand principle
a moment's relief
cleansing water
loved ones holding space

what it takes to call a storm
behind a counter
all kept
steel grates
for your protection
for your domination

the cycle erupts again
you beat me into submission
but I can't stop screaming
and putting out fires
while I cry myself to sleep
and escape to my dreams

Ecdysis

Someone asks
so I speak without thinking.

A snake with skin after skin
in constant metamorphosis
shredding and shedding,
my fragmented scales litter
the carpet of every listener.

Take another toke.
Ignore my asthma.

Integument is an intricate thickness
that I don't understand thru
a dozen moultings.

I speak
without
trigger
warnings.

A friend sees the length of my body,
estimates the time it will take
to moult this layer away from me
but is about to learn
the scraps are longer than neck
to toe to tale.

My ramble is ADHD
stoned nonsense.

I am over-self-   medicated
and in denial.

Opposite   to tail, my slit-eyes
cannot see my exfoliation
through the milk leaking   from.
My friend cannot foresee
how the serpentining   stories I tell
will result in my fangs   striking their flesh.
just instincts   that lunge in pain as   the skin pulls
from my eyelids   and the venom releases   from serrated
and I do not see yet
another friend again.

I meant to let this go   intact.
One whole narrative.
Two-Head understands me.
Ouroboros   got nothin' on how   I will
eat my own shit
and I got nothin'
on how Jörmungandr will   hold the ocean
for time beyond time,
but alone and writhing,
I still don't cry for a decade.

Of Unclean Chimneys, Grenades and Dominoes

When the phone vibrates with hurt
                    feelings
ungrounded, voice raised from *Hello,*

my rage needs an escape-vent,
                    a chimney,
something to let it out.

When the brick chute clogged, pressure built,
                    the smallest cracks
manufactured this explosion

into an upheaval of blame
                    like a timed detonation
of neglect. So, I pick up the phone,

in my self-propelled ignition
                    vocal cords
expelling dirty shrapnel

exploding with *You, you, you.* She
                    covers head and neck
with armfuls of apology, living through an earthquake

drill. *I'm not done.* Three syllables of
                    chain reaction,
and I am the catalyst,

the chemical, my own
                    domino falling,
pressure expanding rapid, breaking

out of my chest and emptying lungs
                    into phoneline
full of rage—

and air. My vocal cords simmer
                    dormant.
Unwitting king of my beautiful rubble, thinking *conflict*

resolved, the touchtone pivots and I am
                    cheerful,
This was a good talk. Yeah? Yeah. Click.

We don't speak again for years.

LAUGH

verb

to show emotion (such as mirth, joy, or scorn)
with a chuckle or explosive vocal sound

"Whether they heard something absurd from an authority figure like their teacher, parents, older siblings, or an officer, he had to laugh."

noun

an expression of scorn or mockery

"It's one thing to make a funny sound, but to *be* that laugh, he knew it all too well."

blah blah laughter medicine, blah blah aren't i hilarious
i forget to even watch comedy, prefer to be angst
then i laugh at myself for my dark
laugh at myself for my proclivities
the more i laugh, smile, giggle
the more i have company to entertain
weird lil nerd-ass jester

and i laugh loud, just like my momma

Eclipsing as Strawberry Moon

I. Waxing

Skinny jean friction
long before skin-on-skin electric
and I was nonetheless
legs tense
          lungs pumping
                    hyperventilated
fifteen-year-old planetoid
in my first-ever cleansing of poverty-stress
through hot months.

The pressure from legs   straddling my hips
and my lunar blood knows I like being beneath
before I do. She's concerned
about crushing with weight
but the more push from   the aubade in her stomach
                    on mine—
          the more I pull her
to further press her warm hoodie   honey eyes
          pheromone-perfume
into my nostrils
                    and further.

My words don't know
submissive
          or bottom
                    or moon
but my noises escape:
                    moans
          or whimpers
of control
          released
in a trust I didn't know

          I gave so freely.

And she is a sun   setting,
the linger on horizon in that skinny jean summer—
warmth held   cooling moments
splattering rose, salmon & coral onto the sky
where I receive light   for one more minute
          and another
                    and another
                    until the earth releases
          her own stored warmth

and curfews pass.

II. Waning

I continue reaching for the sun
    in every second,
cradled by the stones of ancient asteroids—

    this pleasure skyscrapes
a golden-hour lengthened over centuries
    with craters to hold this light

and I will be crushed,
         pinned
         under
    the weight
of our strawberry moon eclipse
by gravitational
         pull
rooting me
to layers of rubble

her sun bearing down

       and down

against my hips

pressed into my stomach.

That Month Post-Breakup

nitakoten ayiwinisa
ekiskisiyân ekwa ninapwekinen
nimiskan wâpamowin
pastipayiw enipâyânihk

          Low-income complex
          party two doors down
and you
          happened to be outside,
and I
          happened to have swallowed
          a mickey of Fireball,
drew myself
          to vomit words
          at the fit of your scent,
          tasting bile in
          the pile of puke
          before falling
to your feet.

And one week after that party
I'm at the foot of your bed
dressed
like I expected to see you, my ex—
pretending
I only threw up tears that night,
and we play-fought
pretending
we could fight
without expressing it through make-up sex:
swallowing tongue
pinning shoulders
dragging me down
tangled in your feet

on my knees pleading.
Oh, to be eighteen again.

to be eighteen again

I don't know how to do this without cliché
but I'm back in that room again
with her in the evening
binge-watching movies
and playing videogames
laying on our sides
and she gets up
and barricades the bedroom door
so no one else can enter
then she smothers me
collapsing
and all I can breathe is her
and all I'm wrapped up in is her

she takes me
and I take her
the popcorn ceiling has seen us
taking and giving
I wanted to thank her
pinning me against the mattress
like a barricade
against the shut bedroom door
except she enters
and suffocating here
she is my last breath

but the dirt in my mouth coughs
into a gasp as we trade places
inside a corridor that doesn't end
in the colour of her brown eyes
and a barricade over the closed bedroom door
but I open and divide synapses
across each inch of her trembling skin
and beneath
this chemical change
cannot be easily reversed

such as that point of arousal
leaving her shaking and wanting
and breaking and falling and smothering
and she can get back up
but it's going to take her a moment
and three deep gasps
before the barricade builds again
over the bedroom door
to give us the privacy
to reimagine the process
in every variety
that makes her feel
airless in her lungs
to bring her back alive
to make her smile
to leave her with that wide-jawed gasp

static energy

Deep brown tones reflect
in your eyes—
a glimpse inside
somewhere north
even a province over
and I wonder what
                    you know
I've never been home,
will it be home?
I hope it's home.
Intuit my way around
sharing poetry for a   lick
of French tongue—blissful
ringing in my ear   wishful
whispers in my ear   your
lips intuit their   way
into words,   press
against mine. I'm   left
pining, right ceding
                              my space, blossoming
sensation in my face
our bodies glance, intuit
                              the movements
                              to open each other
                              up, and in this
                    leg-twisting experiment,
you take lead—please.

Please! If I am ram,
you bull, let's charge
          static energy into another—
I know you'll win—I'll try anyway.
If you are crab rising
and I archer,
my guard is down, and I'm down
for your pincers
          nip, scratch, clamp.
          These stars' stories
map out the landscape,
and I can't keep up.
Stop a moment.   Breathe.
Try to resist, fail,   kiss.
You have to   *go,*
I should let you   *rest—*
but the clock's hands fall off
to grace my body for hours,
we discover tattoos' stories
                    across galaxies
we never expected to see.

Did U Even Read My Bio?

U could date me. Dene, Cree & 6′ 3″ or 6′ 2″ depending on who's measuring. We'll get along if you can agree we live on stolen Native land. Swipe right if you don't mind the sucking noise from my vape mod of frosty strawberry plumes. I make a mean chicken dinner with root veggies thanks to a then-partner I'm still tight with, all squirrel and nut. I also make a decent ramen in half the steps, sans the pork, thanks to delish dot com: fourteen (14) boiled eggs, three (3) litres of chicken broth enhanced with bouillon, steeped with fourteen (14) dried shiitake mushroom, kelp and bonito flakes, seven (7) packages of those magic ramen noodles and bam, seven (7) servings for days. I've had various dating apps for seven (7) years and only a few more dates than years. Is it a race to who's dying most to ghost? 50/50 chances. No one uses PlentyofFish anymore—it's time to see the lack of fish in that 90s sea turned tailings pond and move on. No hockey. Do you like videogames? I usually keep the stress-gaming out of my profile since I don't even like most gamers but I'm on a journey of self-love, baby. Did I mention I'm a poet? You probably think that means I'm lazy or a weirdo, but like Rory Ferreira, *I have this fuckin' poltergeist that forces me to write, nightly*. Did it so good I netted a grant to build this poem and my lonely queen-size bedframe. I get that it's Vancouver, but we probably won't get along if you consider craft beer to be a defining interest. Oh, and I'm an Aries sun, Scorpio moon, Sagittarius rising. I will boldly message first, get protective of my spirit, and fire a grappling hook the fuck out of there. I mean I am looking for something serious, but we could probably still hook up and awkwardly follow each other on Instagram for months after. NO HOCKEY. Do Conservatives use Bumble? Swipe left if that's you. I heard the word *if* supposedly ruins a poem but OKCupid crashes without *what if*. Like, what if land protection work and the journey 'til I die to learn to decolonize didn't clash with my love for medieval fantasy, historical fiction and sci-fi? Did my people ever want to fly or cast spells or create magical kingdoms? Do you struggle getting out of bed? Is anyone *really* neurotypical these days? Don't @ me just to argue. I used to send intentional first messages responding to your profile but too many went unanswered, so I dial it back. What's my personality without a screen to type on? In a pandemic? Without caffeine-buzz, it becomes hard to emotionally justify being too busy to actually reply to your messages. Yes, it's Vancouver, where transit even runs through the rez, but I'm still learning to drive—for my sake not yours. Not a dog person but some of my best friends have dogs. We have a cat, just without the responsibility—the neighbour lets him roam the hallway into our apartment. House plants aren't bad, they remind me that I'm not the only thirsty beansprout in the apartment. I wish I was a cactus so I could be filled with minimal water and conserve it. Instead I'm 90% water, the result of millions of years of evolution and at the end of the day I'm still swiping on Tinder. Coffee is a great first date.

Bird Thoughts in an Empty Room

Duvet blanket and pillows in heaps
with no cool side left
and a lamp lighting the inside
of translucent stone—

on my side, legs curve with
enough space to hold her
across provinces and prairies.
I can see her in the grooves
of lake against land
from airplane window.

I forgot to call my spirit back.
It took forever and the week
to rip him out of Calgary—
they know spirit travels by borealis
and I wanted them to come too.

Long kisses arouse curiosity—
dropping them off at the front door,
and I still wonder what their softness would be
on my cheek, along bone to collar
or a hug longer than a fractionated second—
bring me back.

Away from lonely bedroom walls
to the warm curl of their lips:
cheekbones and smile
illuminate city streets,
they heat homes and pour deep,
deep inside–
bring me back.

To coiled legs and chests in tectonic friction
our planets collide in exploration
of new worlds carved from two.
Our landscapes coming to conclusion
if it'd but fold this continent closer
bring them closer
bring me closer
and make this dream come alive.

To feel the rhythm beating
through their chest—
blood pulsing for the both of us
and how hard it pumps.
It's a wonder we're so soft
with the torrential downpours
in our quaking hearts
and I wanna feel the tornado
of tingles and shivers
blowing in my ear—

I want them *bad.*
Yes, in that sense but this one, too:
back facing me in bed, shoulder rub
galaxies gather in constellation,
conversation,
how can I make this happen soon?

Crackling paper under pen,
I write lines like I'm in detention:

I won't leave again without kissing you.

I won't leave again without kissing you.

I won't leave again
without kissing you.

Wishing After from a Derelict Room

It has been five centuries
since your fingertips traced
the ridges edging my cheekbone,
since you made me stop wishing
that the ship had sank
before anchoring offshore.

The land has known peace and war:
great steel pipelines laid
and a bus lane connecting
my jawline to yours.

If you find this,
there are no more apologies
only gratitude to know you.
If you find this
then tongues open mouths and iron cages
to taste teeth and

cold black air, streetlamps with their orange glow
illuminate snow and ice against riverbank
steaming hot ears freeze in the mist from breath.

I invite the winter in for four decades of dark
to be seen through my frosted eyelids
over three moons and then blink icicles
accompanying trolls beneath a bridge.

If you find this,
winter roads last all year
while light lengthens our stay.
If you find this
underneath your covers
it will be a fur to press upon your neck—

I claw at my own nape in the night
where memories fade from stained skin.
Sharp blades erode a summit's face
to mountainside to cliff-hang,
wrists interweave a pull between us both.
I hold your weight and you hold mine
we hold ours, lips' anticipation
interlock into an entrance
held open as the wolf's hour's candle
wanes to wax where the drips belong.

If you find this
then you've found me
in your lap with temple on thigh

on my side I could stay for hours
until my hair grows into vines
wrapping around your calves.
My grasp is tight
and soft green moss
soaking you in.

If you find this
the only end I crave
breaks provincial distance.
If you find this
my spine, it straightens
each vertebra aligning across your palm

while bedsheets and these five centuries
release from your opened fist.

WHISPER

verb

speak very softly using one's breath without one's vocal cords

"When they were whispered to, it never felt violent, and often tingled the nape of their neck."

noun

a soft or confidential tone of voice

"Sometimes, he could still be loud, but the expectation the secret is not shared was felt like a whisper."

i swear i can't whisper
whenever i try to
no one hears me
so i whisper a little louder
and then the teacher hears me
so i just whisper to myself
mutter under my breath like my father
curse words in Hungarian
what the actual fuck
out of my lips seven times a day
inaudible

Pick up

She and I just head-butt and no one wins.
Crouching beside my queen-sized box spring,
twenty years old, opening the dresser adjacent.
Packing garbage bags: pants, dress shirts, t-shirts—
I'mma grab my TV and get on out of here—
a collection of BC Liquor Store boxes
fifteen-hundred dollars saved and I'm set.
I'm finally moving out.

Mom grimaces, laughs.
You can't take that, and that, and that.
I just gotta go.

I stand,
Fine.

I finish packing, her face unfazed:
Door's that way, I remember.
All I needed was to leave.

My friend's grandpa waits in his truck outside,
my boxes leave out the front door,
my feet make it too, this way.
Had to do it.
Despite me rising to stride,
Momma still hugs me wide,
ignoring anot(her) smirk.

I can go anywhere.

Three Rs

Venomous yellow-green spit, acid rain
from my mouth of man-made tailings pond
all barbed wire and searing wet runoff
            corroding fertilized soil.

Call it justified. Fault lines point
to a country built over Nations.
Cloned seeds suffocating nutrients.
The truth is it's not untrue.
The blame always goes to the state,
easy, now, to speak of disrupted lineage,
fractured continents and what's gone.

Responsibility is a tangle of brown roots,
a word I learn of:
three Rs in grade one.
Just that colonizer's tongue if you ask me.
In university, learn about the four Ds
of Natives in the media,
drumming, dancing, demonstrating, *dead.*
Adorn myself green camo, smile bright
confuse anger with aggression,
what's needed with what feels good,
what's right with what feels right
and learn my own Rs.

Refuse, the first R,
          to acknowledge
          What's right is rarely easy,
dirtying hands to plant ancient food systems,
being accountable to self and to dear friends,
instead dismiss it as a Bible study lesson
and I buried my rosaries long ago.

Rage, the second R,
          when too much
                    turns numb
turns key to lock myself indoors:
maximizes efficacy of ADHD medication
by playing videogames for twelve hours straight;
turns young adulthood decrying whiteness
yet hole-punching drywall like white boy
and refuses to acknowledge the dissonance
in ingesting orange synthetic pill
for grey manufactured problems
when the solution lay in cultivated garden.

Reap, the third R,
            appears foreign
but we were sowing crops all along
the trail
for easy reach
in continuity with the trees,
maximizing efficacy of soil & seed—
instead, assume *reap*
means overharvest,
means grim & scythe & hood,
but fail to notice I've been sowing
the result of three Rs right into

overreaction

collateral damage
self-sabotage

conjuring acidic rainfall
with harsh words
from tailings pond

corrupting connections
with careless actions
all about extraction

and corroding relations
with rusted silence
from radiation

without realizing:
resistance—
hailstorms end crops but some inevitably survive;

resurgence—
surviving crops bear fruit to feed the need
until abundant seasons return;

responsibility—to be that crop
isn't burden
but cornucopia,
isn't frail stems and shorn leaves
but established root networks waking
to thicken, grow, replenish.

Monocrops and sterilized soils
quickly become desertification.

While three sisters planted
strengthen substrata
and when heeding their natural lessons:
feed, spread, climb.

Boy

after Alessandra Naccarato's "Girlhood"

I don't have the patience to burn ants in a magnifying
glass low-income townhouse; my parents throw stones
and put-downs as though they'd been repeated to them.

Their lives, eating magic beans and teaching me debt.
From my throat sprouting beanstalk, climb outside my head,
find myself disappointed in no cloud-borne city of gold

waiting for me above the village. Unnoticing of stars, I tie wire
to my skeleton, electrify the marrow to produce a surge-protector—
I knot myself to the technology of giants; a battery dependent

on a circuit board I surrender my mind to.

Understand, the name passed down to me had meant nothing:
a collection of Hungarian markings on my Anglicized tongue.
The closest translation I found for Bige was *crumpet* and *girl-like.*

My mother cuts my hair to remind me it needs cutting.
Growing out this tangle of vine and cord to descend from the sky.
I dye it blue-black without permission and wear hand-me-down

skinny jeans. Understand, low-income complex means a life,
borrowing, I inherit a feudal system, which like serfs of former ages,
I won't afford. A lifetime of late rent. I think the land might forget

but I'm the new memory, here. I see my first coyote ever and don't
approach. Just witness baring fangs and pawed pavement
from twenty metres back. The sun threatens to rise;
the coyote returns to the bush. I let out a soft scoff in a parking lot

outside of the Newton Real Canadian Superstore.

Mending Friendships

nitakoten ayiwinisa
ekiskisiyân ekwa ninapwekinen
nimiskan wâpamon
pastipayiw enipâyânihk

I do not see my friend for three moons.
Orcas have died   in the plumes from gas
and unreturned salmon in separated seas.

I nursed and grew attached
to a curable but lethal infection.
My friend used to nurse me,
coax me back from ragged breaths
with spells known to the daughters
of Asclepius. They came at a cost.
I cough asthmatic and tell myself
There's a problem.   I tell
my newfound comfort, self-pity,
You're killing me.

White doctor prescribed Promethean pain,
chained to a rock at sea.

My recovery was not quick.

I know I must ask—

glide from seaborne shackles
bid my Hades farewell,
in preparation   for her answer

or the lack thereof. My eyes burn
as they open   from beneath the tide, see
the sun through stained glass liquid, bubbles
float to the surface   where her figure
appears at the edge of the beach.
She pulls me out   coughing,

I ask my friend,

Can I match your spells
or the heart it took to cast them?

She hesitates,

I'm only here because the closest to home I can get
is being close to water.

The waves foam
a final Poseidon on the riverbank
but after she swims,
we shake off the sea.

Sanctum

after Julian Randall

It went like this: I became stuck in that room. When I say, stuck in that room, I mean the room was all holes. I wasn't crawling out of the holes, I was rummaging a maze of tunnels—my grief, stricken long before I lost my brother. I scoured drywall cavern through 'til then. Hit me about five weeks in—I wasn't going to pass my classes, though I always took my meds. This basement suite: my mansion, the playhouse, a home for this clown. I could tell the October day by the sticky taste of lemon haze from my orange pipe; **I held my breath** for two years underground. I lived behind the cemetery, and below. The room turned grave; I slept. Depression: in bed, on the computer, with friends or playing games. Manipulation: **she only climbed into this hole with me** for so many repeated visits before I made her leave. I coughed more than I admit. With anyone in this hole with me, **I realized how little I wanted to remain.** Stopped dreaming; fantasies blinked on computer display instead. At night, streetlight fell down tunnels, pebbles, oak planks, ricocheted off **windowsill and** into **blinds**. I'm trying to say this underground, darkened, was still alight. Though, I **remember** power outages that lasted **weeks**. **I praised** the dark and slowly asphyxiated, **rubble fumes** thick on tongue and nostrils. The day only ever came in streaks of momentary blue. So, with at least a pack of cigarettes per day, **I held ceremony** embracing night. Plastic Safeway bag filled with butts and ash, gathering monument in the corner of the room. I dug deep using a rotation of shovels: **videogames,** cannabis, Dexedrine, sedatives and faithlessness. Couldn't respond to **texts or** call **my sister** back. Dropped **my classes** online, without leaving the pit. My funding cheque arrived for November; they didn't know. The valley **between spine and shoulder blade** felt sore again and again. Why was I majoring in information technology? At a young age **I dreamt** of living in a hole. Instead, sputtered life into a nightmare. An agoraphobic labyrinth I both transformed into and was trapped **inside** of. **The** gravel **rattling** unearthed my lungs gasping when I was excavated from those holes, and I cried dust, and dust, and dust.

Square Footage

I did not come here to bite bullets
        or pine for what's left

over. Rain-city is cloud-cover and wants me
        to live in a closet in the metaphor

and the $1300/month converted closet *1bdrm.* I won't
        surrender my desk and queen-sized bed

for what doesn't fit. Even with a person I love I cannot
        shed the *too much* that won't fit into their *expect,*

already said, *I cannot fit into a closet.* Not a pile of bones
        or a special occasion dress or finance folders

to be hidden, stored, filed.

(Un)lock[er]

The tall locker beside my bunk is empty. It contains bread I refuse to eat, two blank-white towels, empty twilit blue cups & bowl, a concrete canteen of sugar that will not set and this journal. Hear the rain drip over air-conditioning. There is nothing in the metal grey-painted iron walls. I cannot fill my grandfather's lanky skeleton into this now comparatively small locker, though his bones rattle me into and out of sleep on the bunk beside that iron cavity. The locker is locked behind my cell door, yet open to my consumption and so I empty myself into each swallowed pocket of iodized salt I become, looking back out from a sheriff's paddy wagon. This container is not the last hollow vessel I will be devoid of, while hollow grey metal tubes make an ink-stained snake's plumbing where once was grey marrow of an also hollow country. I sip purchased Nestlé hot chocolate, admiring the art of postcards adorned with the images of once-filled Nations that cannot be wholly emptied. White shine moments later—the moon—a guard's flashlight—the empty gesture, not to ascertain my body's location, but to force my spirit from dream, back into that body. Blessed, I had already arrived and seen him.

The single wooden staff posted in a cemetery of crosses on Dehcho land—I just visited is Setsi's filled grave. I return to a blank, grey rain-filled night beside this locker. In a place so full of empty, I see what fulfills it. I smell sweet water on cement. Witness a flood closing in.

ACKNOWLEDGEMENTS

Jonas Bige, my older brother, who made the cover art for this collection.

Kachina Bige, my older sister, and her family who have been an anchor for me in stormy weather.

Darlene Willier, nimama, who taught what little of Cree language I know, and has always been so patient in my journey toward reconnection.

"another poem about not getting out of bed" was first published in *pulp MAG*'s September 2020 issue.

"Attention Deficit" was first published in the *Fiddlehead*'s April 2021 issue and republished in *Best Canadian Poetry 2023*.

"sâkahikanisihk" was first published in the *Polyglot*'s October 2020 issue.

"Ending Friendships" was first published in *Salt Chuck City Review*'s September 2019 issue.

"Mending Friendships" was first published in *Contemporary Verse 2*'s August 2020 issue.

"static energy" was first published in *pulp MAG*'s September 2018 issue.

"rosaries in hand" was first published in *Poetry Is Dead*'s final issue, October 2018.

"reading comprehension" was first published in *Yellow Medicine Review*'s June 2018 issue.

Both versions of "Sanctum" are after Julian Randall's "Palinopsia" from his collection *Refuse.* I have to acknowledge how genius the form of poetry Randall created was, and how inspiring it became for further poetry. Its first version was first published in the *Malahat Review*'s January 2021 issue.

"Boy" is a poem after Alessandra Naccarato's "Girlhood" from her collection *Re-Origin of Species.* I need to acknowledge such an amazingly prolific poet who continues to inspire on basis of vulnerable storytelling hinged to repairing our relations with the land.

For WJ Kehewin who directly mentored me in the creation of this collection, was compassionate and keen in her editing and prompted me toward further poetry to eventually write two full collections.

For my mentors and peers, Nicola Harwood, January Rogers, Stephen O'Shea, Rita Wong and RC Weslowski whose letters of reference contributed to two Canada Council of the Arts grants for this series.

For Aislinn Hunter, Jen Currin and Billeh Nickerson, whose mentorship brought many of the poems that would be in this collection, along with the key concepts that allowed me to stay with the voice.

For my best friend Chelsea Franz, who steadfastly remains in my corner and inspires me to make amazing art, from undergrad to now.

For the generous funding of Canada Council of the Arts, whose two grants allowed me to create this series of collections in 2020 and 2022.

ABOUT THE AUTHOR

Photo credit: Megan Naito

TAWAHUM BIGE is a Łutselk'e Dene, Plains Cree poet. Their Scorpio-moon-ass poems expose growth, resistance and persistence as a hopeless Two Spirit Nonbinary sadboy on occupied Turtle Island. With a BA in creative writing from Kwantlen Polytechnic University, Bige has performed at countless festivals and had poems featured in numerous publications. His land protection work against the Trans Mountain pipeline expansion led him to face incarceration in 2020. Bige's debut poetry collection, *Cut to Fortress,* was published by Nightwood Editions in 2022. They reside on unceded Musqueam, Squamish and Tsleil-Waututh territory (Vancouver).